Into Another Time

INTO ANOTHER TIME
GRAND CANYON REFLECTIONS

Poems by Margaret Randall

Drawings by Barbara Byers

Happy 20th anniversary
Riley and Deborah
from Margaret + Barbara
Namibia, 2005

HAPPY 20TH - GOOD TO
KNOW YOU. BARBARA

WEST END PRESS

Acknowledgments

"Time Changes," "Tough petals sustained," "There is a river," "When I look from one perpendicular," and "Our anniversary" first appeared in *Coming Up for Air* (Pennywhistle Books, 2001) and then in *Where They Left You for Dead / Halfway Home* (EdgeWork Books, 2001). "Canyon Food" first appeared in *Hunger's Table: Women, Food & Politics* (Papier-Maché, 1997).

First edition October 2004
ISBN: 0-9753486-2-0

Cover painting: *Grand Canyon*, acrylic on paper by Barbara Byers
Book and cover design by Nancy Woodard

West End Press • PO Box 27334 • Albuquerque, NM 87125

for Jane Norling

Contents

From the Past

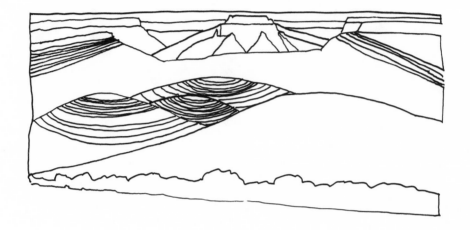

Time Changes

This week, reduced to the rapidity
of surprise,
ends almost before it begins.
I do not speak of measurable time.
Yes, I do know Monday defeats Sunday,
Tuesday rounds the inevitable turn
in the road, and Wednesday
crests the mountain ridge
as we fall backwards
towards week's end.
Action slows then speeds
like the small wooden boat
as it slips off the tongue of water
into the churning rapid.
I am talking about time
moving too fast for comfort,
altogether now,
and salty, not sweet.
Or perhaps it is the other way around:
each gesture so mindfully sweet
that I stand
here turning it in my hands:
bereaved, astonished.

Tough petals sustained

—for Kathy Boudin

the woman living here. Birthing again
this body: once tender girl-child
growing to battle legions of hands
each threatening love or greed,
making her way past tired ghosts
who raise new barricades, fences,
tricks, false promises, prisons,
pits still draped in a stagecraft
of enticement.
Years marching against road blocks.
Succession of lures.

The firstborn. Great hoards of lovers
straining for air and real food.
The daughters. Canyons and rivers
where colors of a setting sun
reach down to meet the body
grown in desperate spurts.
Bridges and storms.
Choruses sung by others.

Petals edge away from the core
where a woman rises. She knows
more now, sleeps from spring to spring.
Sons and daughters give birth
to sons and daughters of their own.
Laughter claims its liquid space.

Now the petals separate
and fall away.
Tender circle of velvet
pushes through this surface
of shattered memory.
New petals: sentinels of renewal
come to support this body
ready to start again.

Canyon Food

—*for Dennise Gackstetter*

The first day I make too much food
you tell me,
that lets people know they can come back for more.
Then they eat what they want, aren't anxious
about getting enough.
I have less waste and a measure of appetites.
Dennise, I have asked for your secrets,
how you learned to cook for 24 campers
forging 286 miles of furious river
through 1.7 billion years of wind and rock,
three thousand of human culture
and our 16 days.

You explain how everything has to be packed in,
all waste taken out.
I have seen each pristine campground welcome us,
done my part to leave them unspoiled
for travelers to come.

I have noticed your daily squares of paper,
lists for each boatman
to forage for boxes of lettuce,
bags of chicken breasts, apples in buckets,
Oreo cookies and cheese,
coffee, vegetables, chocolate, clams.

Mike growing sprouts in the bottom of his dory.
Mary hauling silver tanks of butane.
The exuberance
of Shawn's fried fish tacos.
Jano putting her lips to a blue plastic toy,
sacred trombat calling us to dinner.

It's all in the timing, you say,
all about knowing how long
to simmer the rice,
when to light fire beneath the vegetables
or set the salmon steaks to broil.
Hot coals cover your Dutch oven
raised on flattened beer cans,
promise of dessert again tonight.

River water filtered through porcelain
when we drink,
pumped into pans or shot through with Clorox
when used to clean the dishes or mugs.
Long metal tables
circumscribe your kitchen,
double as hatch covers
waiting as backboards in case of emergency.

It's all in the timing, you grin.
And I know you mean
this mammoth scale
slowing us down
allowing us to drift
from the constraint we call civilization,

trusting ourselves to fall backwards
into our deepest appetites.

" ... the way in which indigenous peoples certified adulthood
was rooted in place. A child became an adult **in a place.** We
don't do that. . . . Education ought to allow for bonding to
the natural world." —*David Orr*

There is a river

charged or gently flowing through Grand Canyon
even when we are not there to view the seam
where rock and water meet. There is a river
balanced by your ache, its equal in every way
but one.

Foolish expectations. The music tells us *sheep
may safely graze.* I too seek that safety, animal
and human, vegetable or sudden raging wave. Now
you are Deer Dancer, dual walking sticks to steady
unfaithful legs

up and across millennia of rock. This Canyon's
bighorn sheep gain narrow ledges, graze
without concern for safety, sometimes fall.
A tumble of whitened bone reveals its story
of harsh terrain.

Days follow water and sun. Nights offer their display
of stars. Translucent walls mass ochre, red, pale
gold, slashed through by unforgiving shadow.
Then comfort spreads her arms. You place one foot
before the other.

" . . . life escapes the broken clay of ourselves, travels away from the center of our living."—*Linda Hogan*

When I look from one perpendicular

canyon wall to another I always think of flying,
half-mile as the crow soars (here they are ravens,
blue-black wings in the highest branches of a tree).
I know the Anasazi tripped invisible hand-
and foot-holds

to mesa top, down to their homes in the caves
or into the narrow granaries. They couldn't have flown
(your eyes incredulous). You mean with wings? No, in their minds,
I say, willing themselves from wall to wall, from Canyon floor
to mountain ledge.

It is what I see. In the magical circle where Black Bear
rears straight up, in that furthest clearing
where residue of fire still crowds to inches of our lives,
I imagine the wings of their thoughts, how they moved
light as the gesture of centuries.

If only your pain could fly, your body let go, unbend
in flight, I would coax the tightness from your limbs,
crack the stories of your other lives, offer
a perfect progression of notes, a gleaming sunrise
for your hair.

"Here you may enter galactic memory, disguised as a whirlpool of sand"—*Joy Harjo*

Our anniversary

is a movable feast. First date, first touch, one night into morning
eighteen years ago. Decision to stay together all the rest
of the time. Then we confessed we wanted rings.
And that's when my first dream opened: a map
that took us searching for ourselves.

Mary Elizabeth Jane Colter[1] called me out of that night, showed me
her buildings of creamy stone, America up and down the Santa Fe,
twelve thousand miles of railroad pushing west.
Early century loner, apprentice to red earth
who made Fred Harvey shine.

Mary whispered in my sleep: we would find our rings
at Hopi House. Bear claws etched into silver. She gave us
the emptiness of an unseen canyon before it wakes to light,
dark shadows pulling me through you to the other side,
juniper circling breath.

Thank you, Mary. They were where you said they would be,
two among dozens, one in her size one in mine.
A dream woven of crossroads and longing. Road trip
spliced with laughing promise, stories without beginning or end,
a code to decipher as we grow.

---

1. Mary Elizabeth Jane Colter (1869–1958) was an architect and interior designer who
understood and loved the Indians of the North American southwest. She produced her
best-known work for the Fred Harvey Company, manager of the most important concessions
along the Santa Fe Railway line when it opened the West in the early years of the 19th
century. Hopi House, the place where our rings were waiting, was built by Colter on the
Grand Canyon's south rim in 1905.

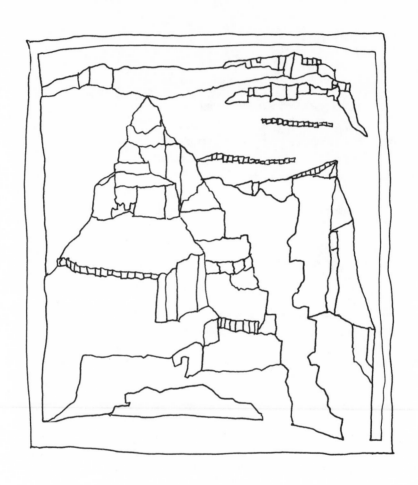

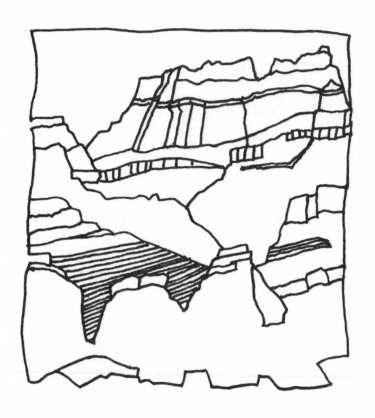

Into Another Time

Get Out if You Can

Great sequences of time,
carved by water wind
and the magic of circumstance,
canyons are slashes
moving deep in a changing earth,
cradles that balance youth's trust
against the center-pole of age.

Folding and unfolding
about our worried bodies
a canyon may be the respirator
that picks up the slack
when human lungs go shallow,
a heart for the cynic
or eyes for the one who looks away.

Io, de Chelly, Copper, Sumidero,
the Grand and all those canyons
that inhabit my parallel life:
it is to you I travel
when sharp edges threaten,
light goes flat
and hunger overtakes my tongue.

In the winter of 1776
something more than Independence
happened on this land.
Franciscan fathers Silvestre Veléz de Escalante
and Francisco Anatasio Domínguez
stood where the Paria enters the Colorado
and named the place
San Benito Salsipuedes—*get out if you can.*

Today I hold your eyes and warn:
Enter only if you trust the tiny flame
that burns in the stories we share,
that place you've lived in
always.

Great Unconformity

Walls of black and rust, orange
and red, delicate creamy pink
and every tone of brown,
green and blue and sudden yellow.
Each purple hue and living shape
sculpts bowls, ebbs and returns,
laps a sheen polished by the power,
millennia of water.
Steadfast schist shot through by pink arrows
straight as my searching gaze.

Yet unconformities, missing chapters
of geologic record
occur when erosion removes a layer of rock
between eons of slow formation.
Grand Canyon gives us
one Great Unconformity
and the Greatest Angular Unconformity:
dramatic examples of this process.

The Canyon as we experience it today
began to form between 1 and 1.8 billion years ago:
close approximation by geology's clock.
Sand and mud accumulated to an unknown thickness,
heat and pressure later turning these
to Vishnu Schist, gneiss, and Zoroaster Granite:
names assigned by modern scribes,
processes we imagine
drawing on every supposition of scale and light.

Between 1.8 and 1.2 billion years ago
the earlier formations became high mountains
intruded by thin white dikes of coarse pegmatite
and thick pink granite.
Between 1.2 billion and 900 million years ago
deposits of late Proterozoic sediments
sat on the eroded knees of mountains.

This is the Greatest Angular Unconformity,
something no longer there,
no longer quantifiable
or possible to assess.
Something we imagine
or cannot begin to imagine.
Not unlike the words *portage* or *decibel:*
absent hours from my speech.

Eight hundred million years ago
tilting and faulting changed the sedimentary layers
into another series of mountains and valleys.
No one alive
can be sure how those rises and depressions
really looked. No tactile animal sense
or human talent
welcomes their contours
through eyes, pores, touch of impatient feet.
Five hundred seventy million years ago
new erosion produced a flat lowland plain
and the first invasion of Paleozoic seas.

What sat and soared
created the Great Unconformity
winking at us now
between the chunky comfort of Tapeats Sandstone
and the Chuar Group: Kwagunt, Galeros and Nankoweap.
Somewhere around 245 million years ago
325 million years of Paleozoic Era
painted the sediment
now fixed upon our eyes.

During this period another lesser unconformity
appeared like a word misspelled,
a letter missing
from the practiced lexicon of life.
My life. How it falters. A slip here,
scratch there.
Reaching for balance, clawing at certainty.
The surface of something, altered.
The moment it takes to assimilate this new place
on the body's map,
unsure it will be there when I look again.

Two thousand feet of sediment rose
during the Mesozoic Era 70 million years ago.
All these dinosaur-age deposits
would later erode
except for the whisper
where we enter this river.
The dinosaurs themselves
occupy our memory,
placed by those who shoot their consumer product
into our consciousness.

From 70 to 40 million years ago
what we call the Colorado Plateau
began to rise
and Grand Canyon as we know it
initiated its relentless journey
into sight and taste and need.
Modern Grand Canyon: 5 to 1 million years young:
its Coconino and Esplanade Sandstone
Redwall and Unconsolidated Dolomites
Muav Limestone and Bright Angel Shale.

A vertical mile below its rim
we invite time and pre-human history
into our hungry bodies,
open our hands, bare our teeth, call out
in a voice too pale
too small too reticent
when faced with the power of mortality
perfectly balanced upon opposing rocks.

At any moment the frustration of a word
forgotten in Spokane,
a woman in Albuquerque moving to place her hand
on the small of her lover's back,
a baby elephant in Tanzania
slipping beneath its mother's swaying belly,
a burst of swallows
lifting off Managua's astonished streets,
the movement of eagerness, hope or critical acclaim
sends a rockslide of change
into the arms of that river.
Altering its shape. Pushing it into tomorrow.

I fix the age to come
beside my moment of witness,
simple cry for help.
Words—forgotten and found—
sift between my teeth,
fall about me
rising and reaching,
freeing both knowledge and doubt,
places I will visit next, click of ideas
settling into the slots
created by my own unconformity:
this passage to next year,
a welcome harbinger of relief.

Feeling and Knowledge

—for Mother, who always wants to go back . . .

I.

The first time I was eight, or was it ten?
Late 1940's, we'd traveled from the east
—my parents, siblings and I.
From its South Rim
Dad took me into the Canyon by mule.
I remember you had to be twelve,
so perhaps I was ten:
two years surely easier to lie about than four.

The Kolb Brothers[2] Studio still recorded
those daily mule trains
as they passed below the lookout point
and sold us the pictures on our return.
For years I kept the matted 8 x 10
—my father's loving face, my braids—
until it disappeared
somewhere between Managua and New Mexico.

Late 1990's I sat at a long table
in the Kolb archives,
my widowed mother beside me,
examining each 5 x 7 negative
from all possible long-ago summers,
my white-gloved hands
fingering every inverse image
containing a man with a hat and young child.

2. Ellsworth and Emery Kolb, born in Pennsylvania, were among the early settlers on Grand Canyon's South Rim. They established a photographic studio and gallery there that began in 1901 and ended in 1976 with Emery Kolb's death. The brothers made the first motion picture of running the Colorado in 1911 and for many years held daily showings of that film at their studio/gallery/home. Until the establishment passed into the hands of the National Park Service, they also recorded every mule train that descended into the Canyon. When Emery Kolb died, his estate gave the Kolb papers and photographs to the Cline Library at Northern Arizona University in Flagstaff.

2.

I didn't find what I searched for
but there have been many Canyon visits since,
too many for my crumbling memory to access.
Spur-of-the-moment overnight with my first husband
in a basement room at El Tovar, mid 1950s.
Taking the husbands and lovers who followed
became a ritual as important
as taking them home to meet the family.

My parents gave me this place
where they honeymooned in 1932,
passed on its power
as example or teaching
then moved us west to within seven hours
of its little rim cabins,
seducing all future visits,
familiar yet newly astonishing.

It's been a while since the last time there
with both of them, we now the guides
on that slow walk along the narrow path.
Remarking on Dad's abilities,
magical vistas eliciting shared joy
until Mom lost her prosthesis
and Barbara ran all the way back:
Please, anyone seen a random breast?

3.

The pilgrimages with my own children:
Ximena and I making peace
in the winter of 1984.
A year or so later Gregory's tall frame
swaying along the narrow ridge,
South Kaibab Trail on mules again,
wind threatening to lift us from our saddles.

Pushing down Bright Angel with grandchildren
more adept by a thousand-fold than I.
Passing it on once more,
one generation to another,
the oldest gone now
and the next beginning to falter,
the middle sure of their children's ability,
the youngest awe-struck, laughing,
February snow and mud
bucking at all our feet.

4.

When Barbara and I were new and
admitted to wanting rings,
it was Mary Elizabeth Jane Colter
come to me in a dream
who sent us to the Canyon, winter of '87.
She told us our rings would be waiting
and as she promised, the silver bands were there:
bear-claw circles,
one in your size, one in mine.
All these years later Grand Canyon
remains our site of celebration,
the place we return
bearing witness to joined lives:
this Canyon that draws me like a magnet
to the shadows moving across its shrouded buttes,
their dawning pinks, retreating stripes of gold,
secrets revealed like prayer beads
one by one.

I celebrate Mary, too: early 20th century woman
who stood alone—architect among men—
countering European style
with the land's materials:
natural stone and wood, Hopi art,
great hearths and a window for every view.
My 61st birthday we paid homage
to all her Canyon structures.

5.

I trusted the mules
before I learned to trust my feet,
vertigo and fear of heights
pulling me back from the trailhead
until the morning you took my hand
and we made it past the first turn,
my breath frozen against fear
then released to new knowledge
opening around the next switchback.

On later hikes I made it to Plateau Point,
the Colorado a thousand feet below.
Horn Creek a rapid I would run
when we rode the river in little wooden boats,
no longer satisfied to gaze from above
but needing to know that place
where wall and river meet,
explore the movable seam
become lifeline in my dreams.

Deer Creek, North Canyon, Saddle,
Nankoweap and its ancient granary
where more than once I've struggled up
the steep trail, braved loose scree
to perch at the edge of time
and gaze down river at the silver ribbon
snaking between those massive walls.

6.

Grand Canyon, I am the woman who returns
to your seasons of mystery,
explosions of silence and light.
What you will not release in image or sound
speaks to me now in secret code,
suggesting a date with memory,
colliding with the absurd idea
that feeling and knowledge are separate.

Around the Bend

It's all about rounding that next bend in the river.
What will engage or assault your eye?

About moving out onto the glassy tongue,
conscious there is no retreat
from the angle that positions
this little wooden boat
for its perfect journey into the wave train,
avoiding the furious hole to our right,
the cleft of rock to our left.
Landing in the current,
beyond the rock garden, clear of the eddy,
integrity intact.

Lean into the big wave, into your fear.
Rise and lunge at the instant,
wave meets gunwale
and explodes.
Its roar of foam covers you completely,
batters you like a wisp of hair
in the swirling vortex of a drain.
Throw your weight
against the power of this river,
doing your part to make it through.

Man or woman at the oars, a body
one with wood and fiberglass
matched to the hydraulics
of a river known like the naked back
of the lover left behind.
The taunt or caress is yours to decipher:
each mole or scar, each hidden rock,
each water level rearranging the map,
hiding or revealing
familiarity and change.

Will Crystal offer a right side run today?
Will Granite or Horn Creek hold us, spin us,
flip us into the thunder
that obliterates the Möbius strip
or release us to continue
this journey that moves
between human and geology,
dory and water,
this question in my heart
its secret place of freedom?

It's all about being willing to accept
what's around the river's bend,
what we cannot see or even feel,
the unknown landscape
offering its hand,
pulling us safely across.

The Terrain

Here
everything goes up:
the nature of a canyon.
And this one is deeper,
more dramatic
than most.

A stroll
up Havasu Creek
requires scaling ledges
of rock,
bordering a narrow path
high above blue water.

To reach
the alcove at Nautiloid,
we hoist ourselves
from one level to the next,
carefully placing our feet,
searching for handholds.

Hiking to the top
of Deer Creek Falls,
in minutes we are
looking down at toy boats
in the river's miniature elbow
far below.

Struggling up
my lungs burn.
Descending
I pull back,
afraid to come down
too fast.

This is the terrain.
This the magic.

Redwall Cavern

At this water level
Redwall Cavern presents
its gaping immensity.
Stories of high-water runs
tell of an insignificant aperture
but today we contemplate
its great expanse,
the cave Powell[3] thought
would hold 50,000.

Powell was wrong
yet it's a hike
from water line
to the far recess of limestone.
Sand moving
from burning to cool,
a place to rest and renew.

Still, it is not looking into this cave
that takes my eye,
embraces my judgment,
for a measure of time
defines where I am or want to be.

I stand in its depth and gaze out
past roof and floor
in the matching black of shadow,
beneath a stripe of brilliant gold
framing red rock and ridged purple
across an invisible width of river.

Inside looking out
I am at the perfect center of my time.

3. Major John Wesley Powell is believed to have been the first Anglo to have completed a river run through the Grand Canyon of the Colorado. A one-armed Civil War veteran, self-taught geologist, botanist and geographer, leader of two expeditions (1869 and 1870), tyrant, later head of the U.S. Geological Survey and expert chronicler, Powell's narrative is the first detailed account of an exploration that suffered extreme hardship, experienced mutiny, and finally—after 95 days—recorded success.

North Canyon

A pool reflects the spread
where rock unfolds,
becoming Rorschach
or the open lips
of a great vulva
traced by centuries of mineral
deposited by water
etching deeper,
renewing itself each summer
in seasonal runoff.

Lips of stone, layer upon layer
of petrified sand and mud
on each perfect but unequal side.
The red-pink sandstone
shelving to purple-gray,
vaginal,
ancient yet virginal
in its proclamation
of birth and wisdom,
wisdom and birth.

Above and below: mirror-images
of one another,
except for the gentle movement
of breeze
rippling water that also holds
a bed of pale green algae.
The lower image is mysterious,
its edges less defined,
its voice speaking a language
we must strain to hear.

Staring at the water I contemplate
the intensity of sky.
My children's births
unfold across a screen
of impassioned fingertips,
pelvis shifting and letting go,
that final push of life.
Gregory Sarah Ximena Ana
are with me now
but do not look back
as they follow their own sons and daughters
away and out of sight.

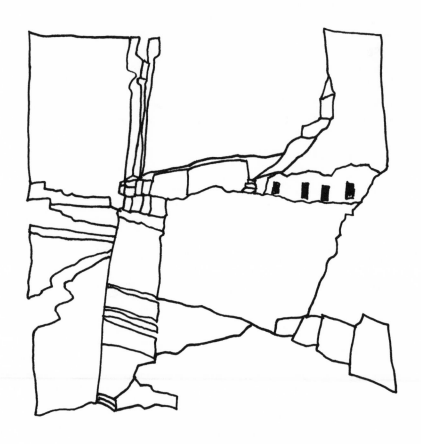

Nankoweap

At Mile 53
another canyon breaks away to the right.
Broad delta, once fertile farmland
where the ancient ones grew corn and beans.
Now a splay of boulders
fanning into the river,
evidence of repeated floods
and other movements of water, wind, earth.

Bright Angel Shale
is about to make its appearance here,
lifting Muav Limestone and Unclassified Dolomites
supporting the Redwall that closes about us
rising from either river bank.
Kaibab, Toroweap, Coconino, Hermit:
formations named by students of their phenomena,
incised and chiseled in pre-human time.

Again to the right
and high in the natural wall: four windows
hard to identify until seen.
Constructed by human hands
at least eight hundred years before,
the Anasazi granaries still try to remain anonymous,
invisible against rock
battered by accidents of wind and time.

Zig-zagging up
to those perfect openings
a narrow trail climbs from among burnt willow
along the riverbank.
It rises through exposed terrain
harsh with loose scree
threatening our steps
as we ascend.

We climb until
balanced on narrow balconies
we stand before these openings in the cliff,
rooms that once held
a succession of winter store:
insurance against sickness,
famine, attack.
A future that would disappear.

In silence
we contemplate the divisions of space,
are made dumb
by the effort of ancestors,
their backs bent beneath the weight
of what nourished and sustained,
their feet rising in continuous journey
from the delta below.

It was here
they put away the grain
that would feed their children
yet their children, finally, ate no more.
The people left,
abandoned these granaries
and the silver ribbon of river
curling downstream and out of sight.

The granaries
are empty now, the people gone.
But their spirits reach out and take my hand
as I begin the long descent.
They stay with me in the heat of the delta
and beyond,
whisper to me
as I try to record this place
emptied of voices, filled with voice.

Bass Camp, Mile 108

Light retreats along the massive wall of rock
pale sculpture of Shinumo Quartzite
and Hakatai Shale
until only its uppermost reaches
pulse in flame.
Burnished ribbon of copper,
sudden spit of gold
racing along their fluted edges.

Massive vertical tipped in purest light,
blinding the senses,
recharging the breath,
running backwards
until it spends itself
in that one last thread
final lick at the edge of time
five thousand feet above.

The dusky face loses its definition then.
Velvet settles into gentle folds.
Shadow descends
accompanied by night's symphony:
cicadas, frogs, the tiny feet of scurrying field mice
and curiosity of ring-tail cats.

Disappearing light has taken my questions
and coiled them tight
in the hollow of my throat.
I touch its pulse
with the middle fingers of my left hand
and remember who I am.

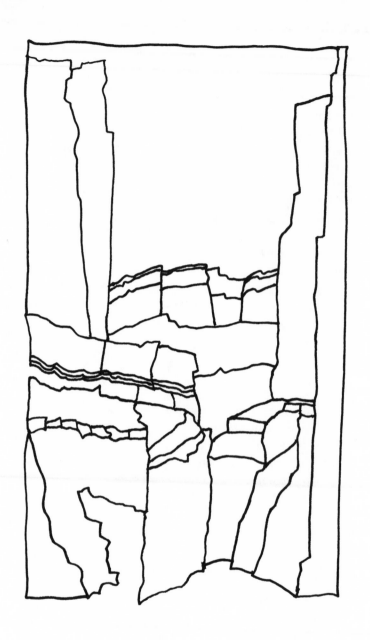

It All Stops Here

It all stops here:
the ravished self
battered by truncated thought
and misplaced words,
bones threatening to crack
beneath the pressure
of reaching and pulling,
concern for that space
beyond the envelope
or inside the envelope.
The withering fears
and everyday dilemmas.

Here sheer walls take over,
pulling me skyward.
The sky itself
narrows to a strip
between their towering heights,
presents night's velvet
studded by distant worlds,
each drawing me
washed and gentled
into its mindless orb.

Here I am concerned
with staying in the boat
as it gives itself
to Kanab's long wave train,
with perfectly framing
the image that claims my heart
or finding a cool spot
to camp along the hot sand beach,
careful to leave no trace
on earth that will host another
when I depart,
bestowing nothing but footprints
and gratitude.

Freeway traffic backed up
for twenty miles,
impossible telephone menus
when all I need is a human voice,
automatons, their arms raised
to position the ringing cell phone,
overkill of noise and filth
claiming the food I eat,
the air I struggle to breath.
All this recedes from me now.

I sit on a heft of driftwood
tossed to this beach
one or one hundred years ago,
allow nerve-endings
to follow half-closed eyes
down river
into another time.
For it is time
that carries us here
more purposefully than space:
non-linear time
coiling to fill the jagged holes
our system's latest consumer demand
leaves in its corrosive wake.

Deer Creek I

Where this river moves
against its wall of schist
one point seven billion years
unfold.

That seam gives
movement to magnitude,
spirit to body,
place to time.

Colors hold stories
just as my heart
in its slowing rhythm
beats against your lips.

High above
where Paiute handprints
fade on the Tapeats wall
their movement of transformation
brings my hands softer, closer,

another river
superimposed upon this one
closing its fingers
over my own.

Deer Creek II

—for Shawn Browning

This time, getting there
requires his steady hand
all the way up.
Pulling, pushing, urging.
Just the right words
telling me where to look
where not to look
where to place one foot
and then the other.

Coming around that jutting rock
on the narrow ledge above the gorge,
letting one eye wander out
over the sensuous swirl of stone
to the rushing water below,
my heart pounds in unrelenting fear
but my eyes sing,
their memory breathing again.

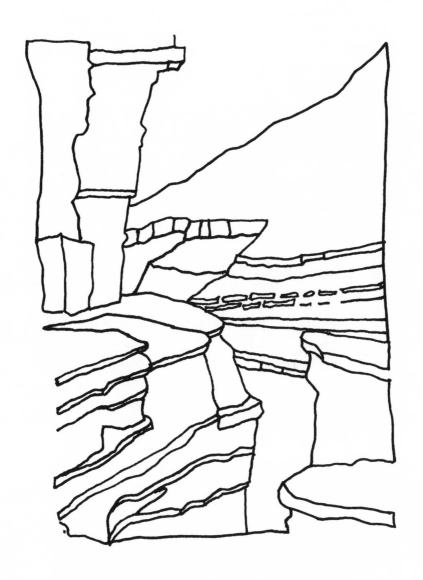

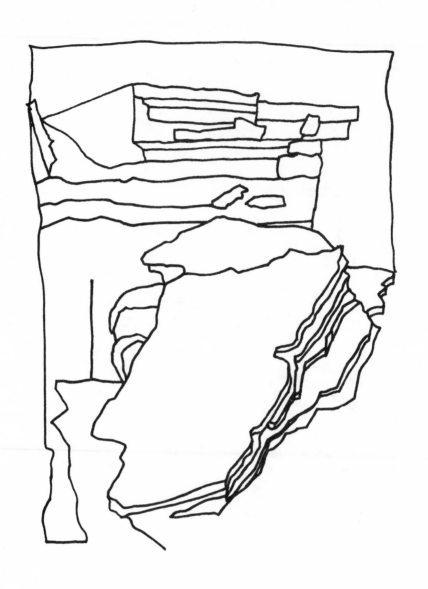

Lower Granite Gorge

In the Lower Granite Gorge
millennia sculpt the cliffs
to this massive sweep
of schist and gneiss.
Undulating landscape
rising and stretching,
opening then folding into itself,
holding us in its riveting pulse.
Symphony of narrow slots
and sensuous bowls
where the work of a stone
rubbed smooth by the constancy of water
carves a particular indentation
that claims the heart,
exuberant and grateful.

Sun embraces this June day
bathing the ancient walls in terrible light,
turning the black to silver,
carving the shadows darker
and polishing the highlights
until a ribbon of riverbank
unfolds in its dance of time.
Look.
The egg-like stone
that carved that cavity
still nestles at the hollow
of its throat.

What appears before us
perfect in its circular story
is a work in progress.
Movement unperceived by the eye
like a gallery environment
in which the artist
is two billion years of weather
and we
who are privileged to know its wonder
are also part of the creation.
Like all great art,
viewer and viewed breathe together
in the perfection of an experience that
defying definition
moves us beyond its name.

The Lens Frames this Image

The lens frames this image
then lets it go
as I slowly sweep walls
that move in the opposite direction
faster than my camera
can do its work.

Panning space but also time:
centuries of buildup,
millennia of sedimentation,
uplift, intrusion, deposit,
erosion, faulting
and the shudder of tectonic plates.

I want to hold the shadow
of an instant gone
two hundred million years ago,
its movement
playing across my line of vision.

I would register this shift of earth,
the roar of boulders
hurtling down a tributary,
the power of pink granite
slicing schist.

I know the camera keeps out
more than it lets in,
obscures more than it reveals.
Only when I lower the Nikon
and free my eye
does light explode
in that crescent of rock,

will darkness creep up
from the deepest slot,
walls claiming one color
and then another
until full circumference
whispers the password
and I move through.

Halftones

If I see the rock walls,
these spires and buttresses
in black and white,
all richness of color fades.
But hue is there, and tone.
Values of shadow.
Intensity of light.
Space deepens.
Texture clears its throat
displaying its brightest plumage.

Photographer,
I have moved
from one medium
to another,
mindful of their
contrasting possibilities.
Now I hold the loss of each
against that which
takes me by surprise
as it rises in the developer tray.

The blacks should be black,
my mentor insisted,
the whites absolutely white.
Cuba, 1978.
He taught me to shoot
without film in the camera,
imagining and reporting
my results.
We made our chemicals
from scratch.

This Canyon defies
thinking in absolutes,
challenges the eye to hear,
the ear to see.
This place invites me
to forget improvisation,
cross and re-cross the bridge,
sending my memory out
in search of wayward knowledge.

This is where my halftones hide.
This is where I embrace complexity.

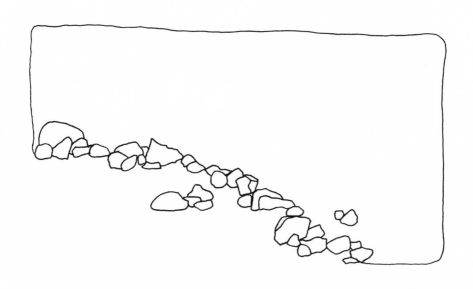

Deaths

This year our Susan died.
Battled leukemia for 16 months.
Diligently. Courageously.
Still died.
Still left a grieving partner, heartsick friends.
Still flares like a sudden ache
without warning or comfort.

Maria died this month.
Her *Times* obituary
told a lifetime of good works,
companion to artists,
artist herself.

Last week
the family we met at Macchu Picchu
exploded against a mountain
after picking blueberries
on an Alaskan lake.
Mother. Father. One of two sons.
The little bush plane
unable to gain altitude.

This afternoon a neighbor called
to thank us for helping with their dogs
while father and brother died
one here, one in Texas.
Father just turned 100.
Brother suffered from ALS.
Leaving within an hour of one another.
We visit
so they can share their sorrow
and relief.

Under my skin
all deaths crowd in
beside that single death:
somewhere in El Salvador,
May, 1975:
Roque, revolutionary, poet, friend,
tortured then murdered
by renegade members of his own organization.
One of those excesses of unequal war
impossible to erase.

Or my father's death,
eleven years now
but yesterday in every soft acknowledgment.
I keep trying to replace his eyes
growing smaller and smaller
as all of him receded
within the gentle man
who shaped my youth and aging.
Goodbye, Dad.

The deaths along this river corridor
come into focus
only because the landscape of their leaving
resides beneath my skin,
behind my eyes,
tangles my thinning hair.

Why is it
I return again
to watch their bodies flail and fall,
grasp at receding air,
go under one final time
when they were unknown to me
in life?

Death pulls us under
rudely or with determination:
a last adventure
filling every door
that waits beyond the coming rapid.

This Is the Tension

Where are the bodies
beneath this swollen surface,
this current that moves us along
at four miles an hour
even when no one powers the oars?

Where the shattered housings
once pregnant with knowledge and dream,
eager for what they would see
around the next buttress of rock
or deep in the approaching gorge?

Many have drowned here,
battered by the never-ending whirlpool,
sucked under in the giant hole,
broken
or given to exhaustion,
carried by a current faster than life.

Frank Brown, whose railroad
would have defaced the corridor.
Bert Loper, who loved this river
and ran its last rapid in his seventy-ninth year
at Mile 24$^1/_2$.
Bessie and Glen in 1928:
honeymooners whose scow
remained intact and without a sign,
their missing bodies still
emboldening river legend.

Bloated or disfigured body parts
lodged beneath a cleft of underwater rock,
caught in the deep brown silt,
buried in the forever of this geology:
as distant from the Colorado's wild beauty
as the life of the African diamond miner
from the woman
flaunting her ten-karat stone.

This is the tension that coils the journey
tight within my breast:
its fierce struggle and silent contemplation,
loss and unimaginable gift,
the feel of your shoulder
against my fingers that know their shape
completely.

Bessie and Glen

Side by side, front-facing
in the last photograph,
she is smaller by a head than he,
her slim body
placed beside his resolute stance
as if begrudging the camera's truth.

His face holds intention,
hers an emotion
not defined by fear alone,
mix of terror and resignation
bequeathed as a final, useless clue.

Hermit Camp, early December:
honeymoon and goodbye.
His knowledge of rivers and disdain for life-jackets
pitted against her love-struck faith,
her need to see an endeavor through.
He won. They both lost.

Their wooden scow
still holding her camera and diary
the box spring she'd fitted between the sweeps
their final store of food,
found placid and empty at Mile 238
its tie-line trailing the mystery
we continue to toss from year to year.

Backwards and forwards
from that winter of 1928,
lives joined in a river
that holds its secrets well.

My own journey between these Canyon walls
tells me risk and obedience
are not the bookends of enduring grace.
Only the will to try.
Only a gesture
beyond that beckoning flick
of a defiant chin.

Being First

How many have experienced this place?
Native peoples first,
those unrecorded in our history books.
Then the great white forefathers:
one-armed Major Powell
struggling to keep his men on board,
old-timers like Nevills and Loper,
and Martin Litton
who fought to preserve a measure of wildness
in a river already cut by dams.

Women?
The first were always wives or tokens:
Bessie Hyde following her husband
in their honeymoon scow;
Georgie Clark, Woman of the River
who built the thrill rigs
that opened the corridor to thousands;
today's women guides
who call themselves boatmen
even as they leave their thoughtful mark
on every river mile.

One hundred forty years ago
running the Colorado through Grand Canyon
was a journey of unknown dangers
and almost certain death.
Fifty years into the past
those who finished the trip
had names, made news.
Today 17,000 run this river every year,
a fraction of the five million
who visit the Canyon from above.

What is the virtue
in knowing a place
no one has known before?
Why our need to be first,
pioneers and record-breakers
at the highest and lowest spots on earth:
Everest's airless summit,
the rumbling crater
of a waking volcano,
an unexplored jungle or river yet to be run?
Mine is the quiet of this hidden alcove
others have seen and left untouched.

Mine the moment, the lifetime, the surface
of this mirror I carry in my eyes.

Not a Spiral

Not a spiral
but circles,
four of them
moving out
or towards their center,
perhaps in both directions
upon the surface of this gray rock.

Someone seven centuries ago
or more or less
held a stone in his hand
(her hand?)
and left this image
that greets us now, oblivious
that others
hundreds of years distant
would try to imagine what it means.

Imagined meaning:
so often the place
where engagement stumbles, falls.

Two Small Islands

Two small islands, polished rock
glistening black
where the river licks their sun-baked sheen.
Splotches of green: reed or willow
cling to soil-filled crevices.

Challenge and dare: to swim
to the closest of the two.
The 50-degree water looks calm
though we know complex hydraulics
roil beneath its surface.

Only with jackets, they say, and only
the strongest swimmers.
Memory of that helicopter's sudden roar
filling the narrow corridor,
searching for a hiker who bathed without.

Two bridge the distance, hoist themselves
onto the rocks from where
they look back at the rest of us,
their jaws forming words we cannot hear
above the river's thunder.

In the channel between island and beach
I catch sight
of the moment we met,
watch as it rises above the surface,
looks my way and breaks into laughter.

Turning back to the beach
I am eager to give you the news.

Where I Am

Suddenly it's no longer about polished walls
changing intensity
as shadows overcome
their layers and verticals.
Or the way light peels
from the highest ridges of the inner gorge
when night comes down.
No longer is it the river
powering from below the dam
crying for its earlier wildness.
No longer the big rapid
coming towards us
as we move off its tongue
and into thunderous waves
that simmer to boils and eddies
where the river continues its journey.

Transported through a worm hole
I find myself in another place,
not unlike the hidden alcove
brushed with its maidenhair fern and columbine,
but also not the same.
For a span of unmeasured time
I know where I am.
Precisely.

What I Hear

Basketmaker, Anasazi, Cohonina,
Sinagua and Paiute,
voices whispering across the deltas,
faint syllables twisted and strained
with the weight of corn and beans,
carried up steep trails
to the granaries they fill
for another winter and another.
Until there are no more winters
and the people too have gone,
leaving us to our clumsy questions
and heartache awe.

We settle into these ancient sounds:
deep shadows
creeping from color to color,
weather on the move
and hiss of temperature
above the water line,
cicadas in symphony
and the ghosts of Nevills and Loper,
the Kolb brothers, Georgie,
the one-armed Major himself,
all laughing as their stories
reverberate between these walls.

The river wraps us in its decibels,
125,000 cubic feet per second
reduced to 8,000 this season
to meet California's power needs.
Glen Canyon Dam adjusting its turbines,
its frenzied electrons
mocking nature
with their dissonant high-pitched vibration,
regulating the flow of what was wild
to what acts without thought of future now,
holding one hand out,
the other behind its back.

As they maneuver us downstream
oars kiss water, slice the calm
of blue-green algae
and white explosion of waves.
This sound too
is woven into a harmony
broken only by the hum
of an occasional motor,
the sudden slam of a hatch cover
hitting deck.
An interlude of thunder
or distant rock fall
echoes our inevitable question:

What would it be like
if one of those epic geological events,
—giant lava or debris flow,
cascade of water
tumbling over the cliffs,
side canyon choked
by a rush of boulders—
happened today
before our astonished eyes
and ears?
And what the sound
if no one listened?

Each river-mile
teaches me to hear
the small sounds
and what they mean.
The chorus of frogs at night.
The bighorn sheep
dislodging scree
from the narrow ledge of rock.
Two desert spiny lizards
softly scuffling their tryst of love.
Full silence
is where I want to spend my time.

Then another sound pivots
and builds.
Breath quickens.
All hearts turn front and center,
all energy drawn
to what we cannot yet see
but only hear
around the river's bend.
Pure power. Relentless.
Granite or Unkar or Hance.
A rapid that shouts its name
in the language of all its yesterdays.

This is the roar that pulls us
out over the rapid's prelude
and into ourselves,
centers us in our knowledge and fear.
This the implacable place
that moves about us
holding us perfectly balanced
in its fierce drumming,
nature bigger than any dream.

We each have our work
at the moment of connection.

My Every Molecule

Pipe organs of tubular basalt
reach high above me.
I lean into their silent notes.
A cross-bedded cross-stitched
swirling layer of sandstone
coils beneath my hands.
Small stones,
perfect beads in a necklace
circle the butte across from where I stand.
Rock juxtaposed like the weaver's warp
overhangs hollows and knobs
polished to a hungry glow
by sand and water and time.
All this embraces me,
invites me to dance on this sliver of beach,
holding my every molecule
in place.

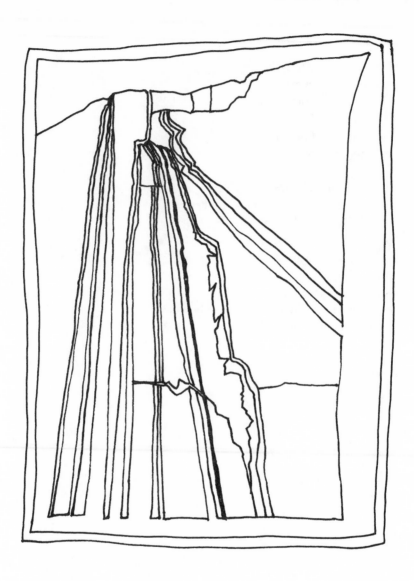

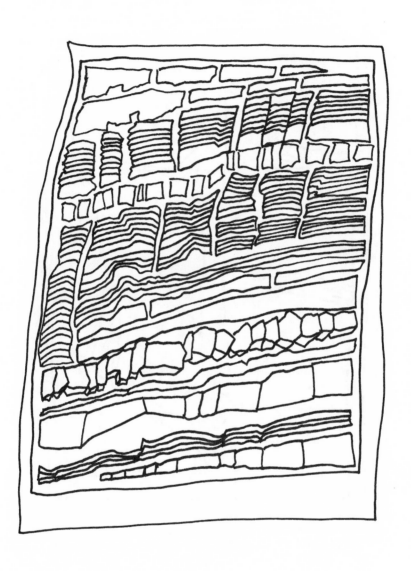

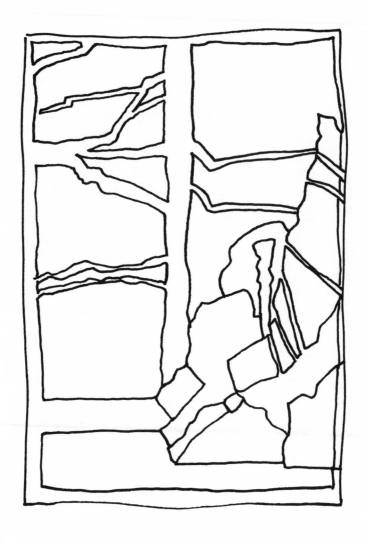

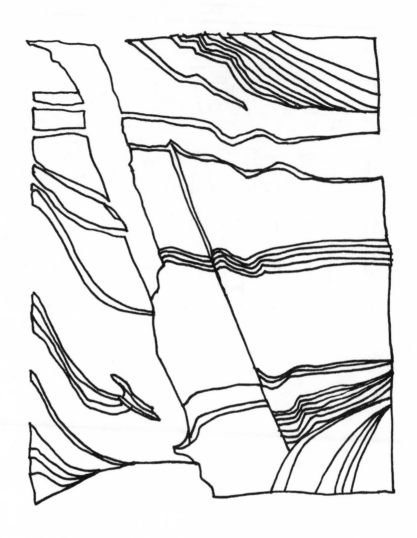

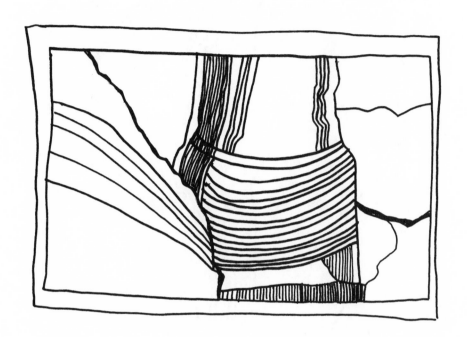

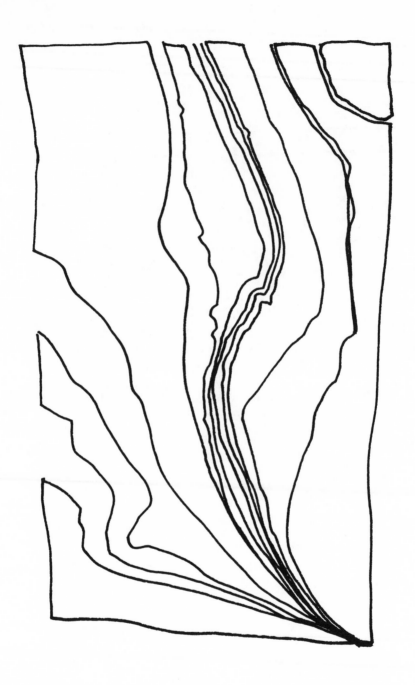

The Notebook

I.

I brought a notebook,
carefully chosen with just the right feel,
a pleasing relationship
between its sturdy cover
and unlined pages.

I wanted heavy paper,
a spiral binding
to withstand the river's wear and tear,
necessary flexibility
when—I imagined—
I would sit on low rocks,
balancing these writing materials
across my swollen knees.

Pen-Tab Industries
produced this particular writer's tool,
100 sheets of 20-pound paper
between cover stock of at least 150 weight,
7 x 5 inches the outer measurement
that allows my book
to slide easily into a zip-lock bag
where a selection of pens
also resist a breach of water.

On my notebook's plain black cover
a seal with the trademark EXPERT
is embossed in gold.
Beside it I added an elegant sticker
proclaiming "Girls Kick Ass"
that one of our guides passed out one day,
imbuing my book
with just the appropriate quota
of belligerence and pride.

2.

I came home
with my notebook empty.
Not a line. Not a word.
Not a quote or point of interest
written to aid my failing memory.
Neither did I make a single mark
in the river guide
kept safe and dry
in the same plastic bag.

Not a sketch.
Not the name of a companion river-runner
nor the number of cubic feet per second
this season's water runs.
No reference to the millions or billions of years
it took to raise these rock walls
above my awe-struck eyes.

The writer wrote nothing:
neither random thought
nor carefully copied statistic,
river story nor important date,
geologic event nor human accomplishment.

Each time there was a choice
between writing or silently sitting,
inhaling this place,
letting it enter my pores,
I chose to open myself,
invite the place in.
Did I know then
I would be able to access it later?
I didn't even ask the question.

A book of blank pages:
the better to see, feel, absorb
that wordless energy
embracing my shoulders,
the sharp pain knotted in my throat
or drumming at my temples
exploding all givens
and spinning me into that place
where I see with new eyes,
hear with freshly-opened ears,
tell the story in a language
that brings the experience back to life.

Numbers wriggle and sweat
in any description of this place.
Scientific names,
geological conclusions,
the suppositions of anthropologists
bear only partial witness.

Rejecting the known language
I begin to create
the one I need in which to keen and shout.

Bette Davis Way Down There

The man and woman stand beside us
peering as we do
over this Canyon's fragile lip.
Deep below
tiny human figures
move like toys
along the down-turning trail.
He speaks to her and she answers
in the softly woven syllables
of their Navajo language.
They point and exclaim,
excitement joining the words
we do not understand.

You offer your binoculars.
The man accepts
and searches their focus.
The distant scene springs to his eyes
and he hands the magic to his wife.
It is family they look for,
family that has left its heavier members
at the overlook.
Then the words *Bette* and *Davis*
short circuit in my ears.

See, there's Bette
way down there,
and the rest dissolves
back into the language I do not know
in the mouths of people
who preceded me upon this land.
More shifting the glasses,
more unintelligible words,
then they hand them back to you,
an English *thank you* as goodbye.

Bette Davis, who looks to be a boy,
continues his descent
in this place where the Japanese tourist bus
disgorges its purposeful crowd,
two German hikers emerge beneath heavy packs,
a child from Peru calls out to her mother
to hurry and see the squirrel
and the Navajo couple lumber off
their large forearms
draped upon each other's shoulders.

Aaron's Cat

Eleven years old and 180 pounds
at least,
you reach out to pull your baby cousin
from the edge of danger.
Sweetness hides
in your Navajo boy eyes.
I wonder what song or magazine story
prompted your Aaron name?

Terminator Two
spews its multicolor rhythms
from the cackling TV screen
in this crowded living space.
When hunger comes
even videos are pawned
if you can bring in 14 or more.
Big brother takes them
on his way to the night shift
at the Taco Bell in Gallup.

Last night your little black cat
died beneath the wheels
of a fast pickup
racing along the highway
in front of your reservation home.
Don't know why I'm unlucky,
you mourn,
that's four cats died on me
so far.

This morning you wake with a headache,
the first of your life.
Winters at school with a sister in Salt Lake,
summers here at Sheep Springs
with a mother who wants you home
and a grandmother
who tells you the stories
she hopes will keep you alive.

In the pan of smoldering coals
we crowd around
one small ember shows pure black.
Look, the uncle father tells you,
your little black cat
and he's okay.
You sink beneath hunched shoulders then,
tears spilling down your young cheeks.

I do not understand the words
intoned in long chant
or the water, feather bundles and prayers
offered to a Heavenly Father
who moves with ease
among the Traditional Way,
Mormon imposition,
and this Native American Church.

Still, I feel included
in the ritual that holds this boy
in the arms of his people,
acknowledges his grief
and asks his mother to keep him safe
from the threat of a life
lost between the sheepherder he will never be
and the violence waiting to take his spirit.

Hope runs unchecked from my pessimistic palms.
For this moment at least
the embrace of a family holds.

Toy

—for Marieke Taney

Gift of the replica
you fashioned from split twigs,
small figure
of a four-legged animal:
bighorn sheep or ancestral deer
who lived in this canyon
3,000 years before we stepped
upon its rock and sand,
its beaches contracting and expanding
with the river's flow.

Wise young woman
on the yellow baggage raft
rowing your first Canyon trip
through this corridor,
your shoulders and back,
bruised calf muscles
powering the long oars, day after day.
I want to be like you.
(Too late for this life.)

More than 150
of these elegant figurines
have surfaced to date
in caves, beneath cairns,
some pierced by twig spears.
Religious art?
Amulet for the hunt?
Navajo poet Luci Tapahonso says
the archeologists feel certain
they were images
of ceremony or ritual.

Then,
remembering her own childhood,
she tells us they were discovered
standing upright
as if the children had just turned away,
as if they would be right back
to continue their play.

She remembers
playing under huge cottonwoods
with siblings and cousins
around the family home.
Doll woman, doll man, doll children
until the doll family
completed itself with a flat piece of wood:
the family car.
Family and animals
loaded onto the wood
going to a make-believe store
beneath the next tree.

The morning
after her dream
eastern sky glowed a clean yellow.
Sun had not risen yet.
From the window
of the hotel where she wrote
the poet could see
the archeological site.

Thin wisps
of fire smoke rose
from the camps of the nearby homeless.
Do the homeless too
hear the nighttime noises
of excavation?
Do they see the spirits
of the Hohokamki being unearthed,
the wandering spirits
gathering with the homeless
also displaced in modern America?

The poet wonders
about her own childhood toys.
Were they absorbed
Back into the soft dirt
beside her parents' house?
Were they carried off by the wind
or by her own children
as generations succeeded one another?
Are they buried now
by seasons of rain, leaves and snow?

Heather was my rag doll
nurtured through a pre-Barbie childhood
U.S. thirties and forties
of the century just burned out.
Then as now, 3,000 years
beyond when the desert children
caressed their split-twig toys.

I told her my stories,
painted and repainted
the turn of her rag smile,
took seriously her desire
which always mirrored mine.
When Heather left
I longed for her face,
its scars a pentimento
like the cryptobiotic soil
we try to leave untouched.

Your figurine
sits on my desk
as I write of this Canyon,
the people who inhabited its mysteries
and their place upon this earth.
How deep is the reach
of ancient place,
how multifaceted its answers
when we must return
to a land where memory lives alone?

(Note: This poem owes a great deal to "Daané'é Diné," from the book *Blue Horses Rush In*
by Luci Tapahonso, Tucson, Arizona, The University of Arizona Press, 1997.)

Indian Discovery

We whose ancestors discovered them
begin our journey through their land.
These pale pink cliffs
are Navajo country,
the Canyon's inner rim
at its highest here.
Indian territory—what is left of it—
stretching lonely miles
into a multidimensional distance.

Escaping The Long Walk of 1864
some hid in the depths
of this Canyon.
I have heard the stories
told in quiet tones today,
nothing to bridge the distance
created by our arrogant history
but eyes that do not look away.

An ancient trail begins in Moenkopi
and enters the Little Colorado
seven miles up the tributary
at Salt Trail Canyon.
Hopi ghosts touch my shoulder
near River Mile 63
where humans once climbed out
of the original Sipapu.

We are reminded of this
just past the junction
where salt seeps from the sandstone,
a thick white crust
dripping and bubbling over the rock.
I look, then quickly look away,
knowing young Hopi men
still come into this Canyon
for the sacred substance.
Our guides do not stop.

The granaries at Nankoweep
are centuries empty now,
no corn or beans
fill their narrow strip of rooms.
But the Paiute still come to Deer Creek
to perform their rituals
where ancient handprints fade
upon the rock.

At Mile 156$^1/_2$
Havasu Creek leads to the village of Supai,
home to the People of the Blue-Green Waters
who once followed the annual cycle
of plateau and canyon.
At Havasu's northern mouth
we cool our bodies in turquoise water,
find diminishing shade
beneath a cottonwood.

At Diamond we watch the Hualapai
inflate their enormous motor rigs
while we try to ignore the boom box
echoing from wall to wall.
Day trips and overnighters,
a people reduced to exploiting
their edge of river,
to hosting the latest motorcycle hype
across a narrow finger of canyon
they bill as The Grand.

We who discovered them
are now ourselves discovered.
History repeated
with all familiar highlights:
religious conversion as cover,
slavery followed by theft
of land and culture,
introduction of dependency and disease.

This Canyon bears witness
to Powell's pioneering expedition
and the three who decided
they could go no further.
At Separation Rapid
they said goodbye to their companions
and were not seen again.

Yet at river level
the bronze plaque proclaims
"Here on August 28, 1869
Seneca Howland, O. G. Howland
and William H. Dunn
climbed to the north rim
and were killed by the Indians."
Today we know
they were murdered by Mormons
but the plaque has never been replaced,
the story never made right.

Indians still come
in search of the sacred salt.
They still climb
to the top of Deer Creek Falls
and leap across the gorge
into another life.
They continue to play their music
down river from Diamond Creek
turning away from that place
where lies obliterate lies.

Connection

Havasu's blue-green roar
carries me far
from the Korean comfort woman
still asking Japan to acknowledge her rage.

Its flow froths over boulders
in this changing gorge.
Ancient Redwall holds me
close to its breast.

Last night's uneven crescent
of star-studded sky
cradles me in negative space.
The stars only footprints of light now
shining through time.

From surface to depth I sink
as Anna Mae's severed hands
thread their warp
over Pine Ridge's upturned face.

I hold out my own hands then,
invite Anna Mae
to follow me
into gentle sleep.

This bend in the river,
these shelves of Tapeats
and centuries-old barrel cacti
whisper the names of Bosnian refugees,
victims of the special tortures
reserved for women in war.

Because I do not want to forget these names
I stand perfectly still
and listen for their syllables
above the tamarisk and layers of heat
rising off stone as old as earth.

The tilted angle of wall
remaining in the ruin of an Anasazi room
offers solace to the tired women of Nicaragua
forced to choose between a fascist
and a man who—once a people's hero—
now answers the righteous accusation of rape
with the stony power of silence.

Canyon within canyons,
place of true silence and renewal,
will your colors imprison me
or hold the embrace that weaves a bridge?

From memory
into the moment of connection:
wings spread broad in flight.
Windows become mirrors.
I open my eyes.

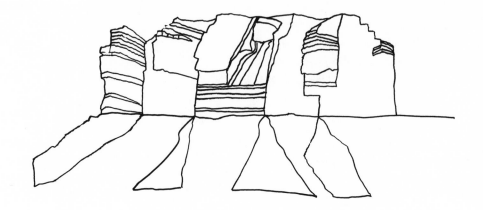

Angles

The tilt of this rock wall
brings tears
just as that other wall at Hovenweep
once made me weep:
then and now
a gesture of return.

There, centuries of tension
between the massive rock foundation
and its Anasazi construction
pulled them apart,
causing the layers of stone
to lean into my sudden sob.

Here, what is left
of a Paiute room
jolts my startled eyes.
Low rocks: loosened by time
and never bound with mortar.
Even beneath this Canyon shelf
the movement of wind and water
shifts its bearings.

Amazement that anything at all
survives.
Yet it is the angle pulling at my nerve,
moving me back
to the map I know by heart.

Silence

In the thundering roar of water,
in the dry up-canyon winds
hissing between these stoic walls,
in the long crescendo of frog song, cicada,
a thousand pair of beating wings
and the songs of other resident creatures,
silence settles
deep as memory.

The electric whir of every known appliance
rumble of cities and even towns,
cough of revving motors, din of traffic,
phones ringing, hawkers invading
the boundaries of our senses,
their cacophony blurred
into one unending decibel—
all are absent here.

Nestled against the backdrop
of that natural symphony:
only the beating of your heart,
only mine.

Edge

Hermit Shale nudges Coconino Sandstone
one edge against the other.
A place
where every sound retracts,
all light condenses,
living on the edge.

In our lexicon those words speak risk, adventure,
a going beyond the expected or safe.
While here, on earth,
edge is the meeting place,
precise moment
between one and another.

You face your wholeness,
I mine.
The edge between us
is stunning and complex:
product of our geology's desire.

Recommended Reading

The following is a partial list of books read or consulted during the writing of these poems. Some are travel guides, some personal narratives, a few contain the magic of literature. All, in one way or another, provided me with maps. The list is by no means exhaustive, nor meant to imply that these titles are the best available.

Grand Canyon Stories Then & Now by Leo W. Banks and Craig Childs, Arizona Highways Books, 1999.

On Foot in the Grand Canyon by Sharon Spangler, Pruett Publishing Company, 1989.

Mary Colter Builder Upon the Red Earth by Virginia L. Grattan, Northland Press, 1980.

A River Runner's Guide to the History of the Grand Canyon by Kim Crumbo, Johnson Books, 1994.

The Man Who Walked Through Time by Colin Fletcher, Vintage, 1989.

Canyon by Michael P. Ghiglieri, The University of Arizona Press, 1996.

Over the Edge: Death in Grand Canyon by Michael P. Ghiglieri and Thomas M. Myers, Puma Press, 2001.

Sunk Without a Sound: The Tragic Colorado River Honeymoon of Glen and Bessie Hyde by Brad Dimock, Fretwater Press, 2001.

Grand Ambition by Lisa Michaels, W. W. Norton, 2001.

The Kolb Brothers of Grand Canyon by William C. Suran, Grand Canyon Natural History Association, 1991.

Lives Shaped by Landscape: Grand Canyon Women by Betty Leavengood, Pruett Publishing Company, 1999.

Canyon Solitude, A Woman's Solo River Journey through Grand Canyon by Patricia C. McCairen, Seal Press, 1998.

Grand Canyon, True Stories of Life Below the Rim edited by Sean O'Reilly, James O'Reilly, and Larry Habegger, Travelers' Tales, 1999.

The Exploration of the Colorado River and Its Canyons by J. W. Powell, Dover Publication, 1961 (republication of the work first published by Flood & Vincent, 1895, under the title *Canyons of the Colorado*).

A Canyon Voyage: The Narrative of the Second Powell Expedition by Frederick S. Dellenbaugh, The University of Arizona Press, 1991 (reprint of original Putnam edition, 1908).

There's This River, Grand Canyon Boatman Stories edited by Christa Sadler, Red Lake Books, 1994.

Anasazi America by David E. Stuart, University of New Mexico Press, 2000.

Breaking Into the Current: Boatwomen of the Grand Canyon by Louise Teal, The University of Arizona Press, 1994.

Woman of the River, Georgie White Clark White-Water Pioneer by Richard E. Westwood, Utah State University Press, 1997.

Grand Canyon River Hikes by Tyler Williams, Funhog Press, 2000.

Down Canyon by Ann Haymond Zwinger, The University of Arizona Press, 1995.

The Colorado River in Grand Canyon, A Guide by Larry Stevens, Red Lake Books, 1983.

Grand Canyon River Guide by Buzz Belknap and Loie Belknap Evans, Westwater Books, 2000.